KU-464-209

Leabharlanna Atha Cliath
CHARLEVILLE MALL LIBRARY
Inv/93 : 2668   Price IR£8.50
Title: CHILD ABUSE
Class: 362.76

Items should be returned on or before the last date shown below. Items not already requested by other borrowers may be renewed in person, in writing or by telephone. To renew, please quote the number on the barcode label. To renew online a PIN is required. This can be requested at your local library.
Renew online @ **www.dublincitypubliclibraries.ie**
Fines charged for overdue items will include postage incurred in recovery. Damage to or loss of items will be charged to the borrower.

Leabharlanna Poiblí Chathair Bhaile Átha Cliath
Dublin City Public Libraries

Dublin City
Baile Átha Cliath

Date Due	Date Due	Date Due

CHILD ABUSE

by Karen Bryant-Mole

Consultant: John Hall,
Counselling Support Manager of ChildLine

Wayland

Adoption
Bullying
Child Abuse
Death
Growing Up
Splitting Up
Step Families

Designed by Helen White
Edited by Deb Elliott

We gratefully acknowledge the assistance of the following people
in the production of this book:
Clermont Child Protection Unit, East Sussex Social Services;
Dr Rachel Waugh, Principal Clinical Psychologist,
Great Ormond Street Hospital

Some of the more difficult or unusual words are explained in the glossary on page 31.

First published in 1993 by Wayland (Publishers) Limited
61 Western Road, Hove, East Sussex BN3 1JD

© Copyright Wayland (Publishers) Limited

British Library Cataloguing in Publication Data
Bryant – Mole, Karen
 Child Abuse. – (What's Happening? Series)
 I. Title II. Series
 362.7

ISBN 0 7502 0498 2

Phototypeset by White Design
Printed and bound in Belgium by Casterman S.A.

CONTENTS

This book contains a number of personal accounts of abuse. We have changed the names of all the people involved to protect their identities.

WHAT IS CHILD ABUSE?

You may have heard the words 'child abuse' and perhaps you have wondered what they mean. The word 'abuse' means 'to use in a bad way', so child abuse means that something wrong is happening.

If a child is being hurt in some way, perhaps by being punched or beaten, it is called physical abuse. Sometimes parents don't know how to, or choose not to, look after their child properly. Perhaps they leave the child alone for long periods of time. This type of abuse is sometimes called 'neglect'.

There is another type of abuse which is often called 'sexual abuse'. This phrase is difficult to explain because it can mean lots of different things. When people use the term 'child sexual abuse' they usually mean someone, like an older child or an adult, using or touching a child's body to give themselves pleasure. It might mean someone asking or telling a child to do something to them or it might mean them doing something to the child. It usually involves the parts of your body that some people call 'private' parts. Different families have different names for these parts of your body. Think about the words you use in your family.

This book is mostly about the the type of abuse which is sometimes called sexual abuse. Sexual abuse can be something that happens just once or something that goes on over a long period of time.

RIGHT *It is not always possible to tell if someone is being abused. If you are being abused please talk to someone you trust about it.*

TOUCHING

RIGHT Sarah did not like the way her Uncle Tom had touched her. It had not felt right.

Sarah often used to stay with her Uncle Tom and Aunt Sue. She had been visiting them since she was a little girl. They weren't a real aunt and uncle – they were good friends of her mum and dad.

Sarah really liked them but during one visit something strange happened. Uncle Tom was reading her a story in bed and giving her a cuddle, as he often did. But this time, instead of just kissing her goodnight, he put his hands under her nightie and started touching her all over. Sarah didn't like it. At first she was surprised but then she felt embarrassed and she told Uncle Tom to stop it. Sarah was confused. Why had it felt alright when Uncle Tom had cuddled her but not when he touched her like that?

Not all touches are the same. Perhaps it would be helpful to try to think of the difference between those two touches. When Uncle Tom cuddled her it made Sarah feel warm and happy but when he touched her under her nightie it made her feel confused and embarrassed. Sarah somehow just knew that something wrong was happening.

There is nothing nicer than a cuddle or a tickle or a hug with someone you like as long as it makes you feel happy and safe. But if it is the sort of touch that makes you feel confused or worried or frightened, tell the other person to stop. If you feel too scared to tell the other person to stop, make sure you tell someone you trust about what has happened.

BELOW Everyone loves a cuddle with someone they like. It makes you feel all warm and happy inside.

SECRETS

Sometimes it can be difficult to decide whether what has happened, or is happening, to you is alright or not.

Mark was being abused by an older boy called Chris. Chris used to come and babysit once a week while Mark's mother did a late shift at work.

Chris was everything that Mark wanted to be. He was funny, clever, and great at sport. Mark wasn't really sure how he felt about what was going on but Chris had told him it was their special secret. It made Mark feel important to know that he and Chris had their own secret. But Mark was worried about it too because his mum had told him to come to her if he ever felt unsure about anything.

A good rule about secrets is to think about why they are secrets. Good secrets have proper reasons. You wouldn't tell your dad what you had bought him for his birthday because it would spoil the surprise. If someone has asked you to keep something a secret, especially if it has to do with your body in some way, ask them why it has to be a secret. If they can't give you a good reason, it would probably be best not to do that thing again and to tell someone you trust about what has happened.

OPPOSITE It's fun to keep something secret as a surprise. But it's often best to tell your mum or dad about other secrets you are asked to keep, especially if they make you feel worried or upset.

TRICKS AND BRIBES

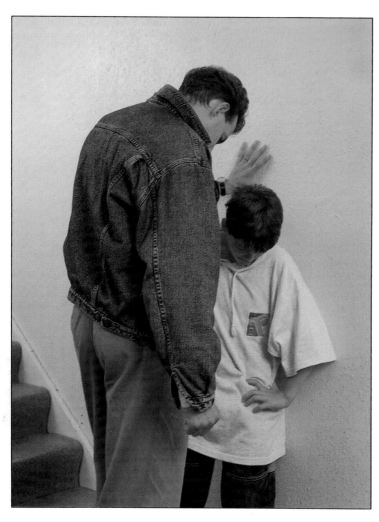

ABOVE If someone has to threaten you or bribe you not to tell about something, then what has happened is probably wrong.

Sean was very good at basketball. Mr Berry, his coach, had asked Sean to come to the practices early for some extra coaching.

One day Mr Berry said they were going to play a really special game. Mr Berry often made up games to help improve Sean's basketball but this game was different. It started off alright, but before he knew what was happening Mr Berry was doing things to Sean that Sean didn't want him to do. Afterwards Mr Berry told him not to tell anyone about their game. He threatened Sean by saying that if he told he would be dropped from the basketball team and he tried to bribe him by telling him that if he didn't tell he could play in every match.

Abusers often trick children by pretending that it is only a game. If you are asked to do something you don't want to or if someone tries to do something to you that you don't like or something that hurts you, tell them to stop and then get away.

If you are ever abused by a person your parents trust to look after you, it is very important to tell someone about it. It is quite likely that you are not the only child that this person has abused. Telling will probably stop it happening to you and it may stop it happening to someone else.

BELOW If someone does threaten or bribe you, tell someone you trust about it.

IS IT MY FAULT?

Jenny's mum and dad didn't have a lot of money, so they earned a bit more by taking in a lodger. But the lodger had started abusing Jenny. She knew that what was happening was wrong, but she thought that if she told anyone about it that person would tell her off and say it was her fault.

Sometimes she wondered if it really was her fault. She wondered whether perhaps she had done something or said something to the lodger to make him think she wanted him to do these things to her. All these thoughts made Jenny feel very mixed-up. She blamed herself for what was happening. She thought about how long it had been going on and she felt guilty because she hadn't told anyone about it when she knew it shouldn't be happening. Sometimes she liked the things the man did but enjoying something that she knew was wrong made her feel even worse.

Jenny blamed herself for the abuse but there is something very important to remember. Abuse is never, ever the fault of the child. People who abuse children know that what they are doing is wrong. That is why they have to tell you to keep it a secret. Sometimes they may try to tell you that it is your fault and that you wanted them to do it or let them do it. But they are wrong. It is not your fault, it is their's.

LEFT *Jenny felt it was her fault that she was abused. It wasn't. Abusers know that they are doing something wrong.*

TELLING

Andrew always spent Saturday mornings with his grandfather. It should have been a happy time but it wasn't because Andrew's grandfather was abusing him

He knew that he ought to tell someone about it but he was frightened about what might happen. Would he get the blame, would the police come to the house, would his grandfather be sent to prison, would he be taken away and put in a children's home?

Andrew felt very lonely. He had a big problem and he was having to deal with it all by himself. He was so

BELOW At first, Andrew would not tell anyone that he was being abused. He was frightened about what would happen.

worried that he couldn't concentrate at school. His teacher asked Andrew if there was anything bothering him. Andrew said no at first but eventually he told her about what was happening. Afterwards part of him was still frightened but another part of him was relieved that someone else knew about his secret. Sharing it with someone else made him feel a little less alone with the problem.

What happens after you tell will depend on who is abusing you and how they are abusing you. Whatever happens to the abuser, it is his or her fault, not yours. They chose to do something that they knew was wrong.

ABOVE Many children find telling very difficult but it really is the only way to stop the abuse.

WHY ARE YOU ANGRY?

RIGHT At first, Kelly's mum was really angry and upset when Kelly told her she was being abused.

Kelly had been abused a number of times by Claire, who was a friend of her mum's. Kelly was scared about telling her mum but she decided it was the only thing she could do because she didn't want to go round to Claire's house any more.

16

Kelly wanted her mum to make everything alright again but instead she was furious. She shouted at Kelly and told her she was wicked for making up such horrible stories.

Kelly was confused. She thought she had done the right thing but everything had gone wrong.

After a while Kelly's mum calmed down. She said she was sorry for shouting. She explained that she wasn't really cross with Kelly but that she was so shocked by what she had told her that she didn't want to believe it. She asked Kelly if she wanted to talk about it and this time she was able to give her the help and love she needed.

If you tell adults about what has happened, you too may find that they are angry with you or blame you. Often they act this way because they are shocked and angered by what has happened. If the person you tell is angry you could try again later when he or she has had a chance to think about it. If the adult still doesn't want to listen, you should find someone else who you trust and try to talk to them.

BELOW Kelly's mum was sorry she had shouted at Kelly. She hadn't been angry with Kelly, she had been shocked about what Kelly had told her.

I DIDN'T KNOW IT WAS WRONG

OPPOSITE Jade had been abused since she was very little. She thought it was part of family life until she talked to her friends about it.

Jade was being abused by her father but she thought that what was happening went on in all families.

One day when she was talking to her friend Nicola in the playground she happened to mention something that her dad did to her. Nicola said, '*That's a funny thing to do. My dad doesn't do that*'.

Later that day Nicola said to her mum, '*Do you know what Jade's dad does?*' Nicola's mum was surprised and asked Nicola if she was sure that was what Jade had said. Nicola's mum didn't know what to do. Eventually she decided to tell the girls' class teacher.

It came as a big shock to Jade to find that what her dad had been doing was wrong. She felt very mixed-up about it all. She loved her dad and had always trusted him. Now she felt let down by him and she was worried that no one would believe her when she said that she hadn't known it was wrong.

Jade didn't know it was wrong until someone else told her. Sometimes children realize it for themselves, perhaps from things they hear their friends saying. They may be confused about what to do. They worry that they will look silly if they tell now about something that has been happening for a long time. They feel that other people will think that they are to blame because they went along with it. If this has happened to you don't blame yourself for not knowing. The important thing now is to tell someone about it. And remember, none of this is your fault.

STRANGER DANGER

Toby was playing in the park when he noticed a man watching him. The man came up to Toby and asked him if he would like a football that he had at home. He said he only lived around the corner and told Toby he could come and get it now if he liked. Toby went with the man but then the man grabbed Toby and took him behind some bushes. The man started to touch Toby in a way that frightened him. Toby struggled and managed to get free and run away.

If strangers ask you to go somewhere with them, say no, even if they look kind. They may try to trick you by saying that your mum or dad said it was alright or by offering you something you would like.

If a stranger tries to grab you or won't leave you alone, you should scream or shout or bite or kick. You have probably been told that it is naughty to bite or kick and usually it is. But this situation isn't usual. You should do whatever you can to keep yourself safe. The attacker won't like it if you make a noise and draw attention to yourself and a painful kick or bite may make him let go of you. If you get a chance, run and then tell someone you trust about what has happened.

If, like Toby, you have ever been attacked, remember that it was not your fault. If you have been attacked but not told anyone about it, it's not too late to talk about it now. It doesn't matter if it happened a long time ago, sharing what happened often helps.

OPPOSITE Toby got away from the stranger. When he got home he told his mother what had happened.

PLEASE BELIEVE ME

OPPOSITE If you tell someone that you are being abused and he or she won't believe you, try telling someone else.

Lisa was very unhappy. She was being abused by her stepfather. It had started soon after he moved in with her and her mum.

In the end Lisa told her mum. Lisa's mum asked her stepdad about it but he said that Lisa was making it up. He said it was just her way of getting at him because he wasn't her dad. It wasn't true but Lisa's mum believed him. She told Lisa she was horrible for saying such things. Lisa felt lonely and helpless. She became very quiet and stopped playing with other children.

It was her grandfather who first noticed how much Lisa had changed. He asked Lisa if there was anything wrong but Lisa wouldn't talk about it. He suggested to Lisa's grandmother that perhaps Lisa might talk to her. Her grandmother told Lisa that if there was anything she wanted to talk about she was a good listener.

At first Lisa just told her a little bit about it. She was scared that her grandmother might think that she was lying too, so Lisa waited to see what happened. Her grandmother looked very serious but asked Lisa to carry on. When she realized that her grandmother believed her, Lisa burst into tears. Her grandmother cuddled her and, crying, Lisa told her about everything that happened.

If you tell someone about being abused but he or she can't, or won't, believe you, you may feel that the situation is hopeless. Don't give up. Think of someone else who might be able to help you. You could try talking to a relative, a friend's mum or a teacher.

WHY DIDN'T SHE HELP ME?

ABOVE Elsa's mum had not known that Elsa was being abused. She was shocked when she found out and felt guilty.

Elsa was eight. She had an older brother called Daniel who was sixteen. They were often alone together in the house. Recently he had started abusing her. When she told him to stop, he said that mum had left him charge so Elsa had to do what he said. When what was happening was discovered, Elsa was asked why she hadn't said anything to her mum. Elsa replied angrily, *'How could I? Mum put Daniel in charge. She must have known all about it.'*

Elsa was angry because she had wanted her mum to look after her and she felt that her mum had let her down. But Elsa's mum had had no idea about what was going on. When she found out about it she felt angry too, and guilty because she hadn't protected Elsa.

Elsa and her mum found it helpful to talk to each other about how they were feeling. Eventually Elsa stopped feeling so cross with her mum.

Occasionally, mums do know what is happening but feel they can't do anything about it. This might be because the abuser is someone they love and they are torn between their love for you and their love for him. It may be because they find it too difficult to think about what is happening and so they ignore it. Usually, though, mums don't know what is happening and are shocked when they find out and do everything to protect their children. It is important to remember that neither you nor your mum are to blame. The blame always lies with the abuser.

LEFT If you are being abused you might think that your mum must know about it and blame her because you feel she should have protected you.

I LIKE ME!

Some children who have been abused seem to get over it quickly. Many children find it more difficult.

Lots of children feel confused about what has happened. Some children feel ashamed and think that being abused has made them into dirty or bad people. They may feel that they don't like themselves very much any more or that other people couldn't possibly like them.

What has happened to you hasn't made you dirty or bad. One way of helping yourself to stop feeling like this is to learn to like yourself again. Think of things you are good at. It doesn't have to be school things. It could be making paper aeroplanes or balancing books on your head!

Think of the people who like you. Even if you think that no one likes you, it probably isn't true. Don't just think about friends your own age, think about younger

All children have sad memories as well as happy memories. The fact that your sad memories might be about being abused doesn't make you different.

children, teachers or grandparents. Knowing that you are good at things and that people like you, helps you feel good about yourself.

Many children feel that what has happened has somehow made them different to other children. The only thing that is different is that they have had an experience that other children may not have had.

THE FUTURE

ABOVE If you are or have been abused, please tell someone about it.

The most important message for any child who is reading this book, is that if you are being, or have been, abused you should tell someone about it. It is a situation that is very difficult to sort out by yourself. You will probably need the help of people who you know and trust or people whose job it is to make sure that children are protected from this sort of abuse.

Telling is often difficult. If the abuser is someone you know or love you may feel that you are letting them down. This is not true. It is he or she who has let you down. Whatever happens after you have told, try to remember that everyone who becomes involved in

LEFT *Being abused doesn't mean you will never be happy again.*

sorting things out will be thinking about what is best for you. Sometimes telling might seem to have made things worse but, in time, most children look back and think that telling was the right thing to do.

What has happened to you is something that you will probably never forget but, when things have been sorted out, it will be something of the past. Look forward to the future.

FOR PARENTS, TEACHERS AND FRIENDS

If a child talks to you about being sexually abused, it is important to take him or her seriously. Children of this age rarely lie about this type of abuse. Telling is not easy. It will have taken a lot of courage to talk about it.

If a child tells you that he or she has been abused you may feel angry or shocked or sickened. Try to remember that it is the abuser's fault and not the child's. It is very easy to take out your anger on the child as he or she is there and the abuser is not. Negative reactions may stop children disclosing the full extent of the abuse and may even make them retract what they have said in an attempt to stop you being angry.

As a general rule, it is not a good idea to put words into children's mouths by asking whether, for example, a specific person did a specific thing. Children may say yes, simply because they want to please you and they think that that is what you want to hear. Allow the child to tell you what has happened in his or her own words.

Many abused children feel lonely, helpless and guilty. A child who talks to you about abuse is attempting to overcome the loneliness by sharing his or her problems with you. Children feel helpless because they can do very little about the situation themselves. A child who talks to you about abuse is probably asking for your help. Lots of children feel guilty and think they are in some way to blame for the abuse. One of the most important things you can do is to stress that you do not blame them at all and to tell them how much you love them. Children who tell about abuse need to be praised. They need to know that they have done the right thing.

What you do after a child has talked to you will depend on very many things, such as the nature of the abuse and your relationship with the child. It may be that you find the problem too difficult to cope with or you feel that you are not the right person to deal with it. But don't just do nothing. A child has turned to you for help. If you can't provide that help, help the child to find someone else who can.

GLOSSARY

Ashamed   To feel very bad and guilty about something you have or think you have done.

Betrayed   To be let down by someone you trusted.

Bribes   Things that people offer you when they want you to do something which is usually wrong.

Concentrate   To think very hard about something.

Lodger   A person who pays to live in someone else's house.

Threaten   To tell someone that something awful will happen if he or she does not do what you want.

INDEX

Picture Acknowledgements

The following pictures are from: Cephas 4-5 (Mick Rock), 24 (Jim Loring); Chapel Studios/Zul Mukhida 8, 10, 11, 16, 17, 20, 23; Jeff Greenberg 19; Eye Ubiquitous 12-13, 26, 28; Daniel Pangbourne 6, 14, 15, 25; Tony Stone Worldwide cover, 7 (Dale Durfee), 26-7 (Arthur Tilley), 29 (Martin Chaffer);

All of the people who are featured in this book are models. We gratefully acknowledge the help and assistance of all those individuals who have been involved in this project.